EASY GUIDE TO DEVELOP AN INTERACTIVE WEBSITE USING CONTENT MANAGEMENT SYSTEM (CMS) JOOMLA

Fellow Webmasters,

This guide will teach you from the scratch how to develop a website using the most popular CMS_ Joomla.

When your client demands a site requiring storing and retrieving data, then you will appreciate the prospects of Joomla.

Joomla is quite very easy to learn and deploy. Within three hours, you can get a Joomla site moderately running. So you do not need to be an experienced website developer to learn Joomla, newbies can deploy a Joomla site within a day.

Is there any requirements to be in this class? None! Anyone who can read this post here and is willing to learn Joomla can grasp it.

So let's get started...

Table of Content:

1. **Overview of Joomla.**

Welcome to Joomla!!!

Joomla is a FREE Content Management System (CMS) that enables you to build world class websites and powerful web applications. Its ease-of-use and extensiveness have made Joomla the most popular website software available. Best of all, **Joomla is an open source**, so it is freely available for everyone to use.

Let me quickly explain what a Content Management System (CMS) means in respect to website development. A CMS is software that keeps track of all the content of your website. Content can be text, image, video or anything you can think of. **A major advantage of using Joomla is that it requires almost no technical skill or knowledge to manage.**

Many Corporate Web sites or portals, online magazines, newspapers, and publications, Government applications, School and church Web sites are running on Joomla.

Some websites belonging to Governments of countries are built using Joomla? That is emphatically true. You can guess what that cost. Funny enough, you can put up such government website running in a matter of hours.

So you are in for something spectacular here.

Next topic loading........80% done!

2. Installing Joomla in a few steps

There are very simple ways to install Joomla. In fact, there are basically two ways to install Joomla.

1. Download a copy of Joomla from http://Joomla.org and install it on your computer offline or on an online hosting server. In plain terms, let's refer to your hosting server as your website running online.
2. Install Joomla directly into your online website using script installer in the control panel of the site.

For the sake of time, I'll talk more on second option. Install Joomla directly into your online website using script installer in the control panel of the site......... and also the later part of option 1. i.e. installing downloaded Joomla files into an online website. The reason is, installing Joomla on your computer to run will require you to install and configure a local server like Apache, install PHP and Mysql. You can download AMMPS (a software stack from Softaculous enabling Apache, Mysql, MongoDB, PHP, Perl, Python and Softaculous auto-installer on a desktop.) from http://www.ampps.com/downloads and install it in your system. I'll talk about developing a Joomla site offline much later in this course.

This Course will teach you the latest version of Joomla which version 3.1.

So let's go to....

1. Download a copy of Joomla from http://Joomla.org and install it on an online hosting server (online website)

Welcome back. We were supposed to learn
1. Download a copy of Joomla from http://Joomla.org and install it on an online hosting server (online website) but on a second thought, lets learn how to use Joomla offline (localhost). This will save cost on the part of a new user and also someone who has no regular access to internet service. Though you'll need the internet to download some applications and files that we'll be using in this class.

Quickly, download....
1. Joomla from http://Joomla.org/downloads.html
2. AMPPS from http://ampps.com/downloads.

Joomla is the CMS while AMPPS contains Apache, MySQL, MongoDB, PHP, Perl and Python.

The AMPPS file is an executable file (.exe). So install it on your computer. After the installation, open its user interface and start Apache and MySQL. If all went well, the afore-mentioned services will start.

MySQL usually does start but you may have problem with the Apache and this usually an issue relating to another port using port:80. To fix this, on the AMPPS user interface, click Apache, then Configuration. The configuration file will open in a text editor like notepad. Go the line 49 of that file and change Listen 80 to Listen 8080, save the file. Restart the Apache.

Open your browser and type: localhost:8080 and press enter. Your system now has a local server that will enable us develop the Joomla site as though we were online.

If you have any issues with configuring your local server. Please you may ask before we proceed.

If your installation of AMPPS has gone as I outlined, by the time you type: localhost:8080 on your browser, you'll see the screen below.

Now that you have a server, let's deal with the Joomla file that you downloaded. The file is compressed so you need an extracting software like WinRar to extract the file to a folder. Let us name this folder as JoomlaTraining. This means all the Joomla files are inside the JoomlaTraining Folder.

Next, you will copy the JoomlaTraining folder to a subfolder called www in your AMPPS folder. By default, AMPPS would be installed to your c:\ drive. This means the JoomlaTraining will be in this path. c:\Ampps\www\JoomlaTraining.

WAMPP and WAMPP will have similar path.

Now lets install Joomla but before we do, lets create a database and a user for the database.

Creating a database:
Open your browser and type: localhost:8080/phpmyadmin and then press enter. You'll have a screenshot as the one below.

Now, in the phpmyadmin environment, click on Users. Then below it, you will see, Add user, click on it. The add user environment opens.

1. Enter User name, in this case let's use: joomxyz
2. Then under Host, select local
3. Password: user123
4. Re-type (password): user123.

Scroll down to see: **Database for user**
1. Check: Create database with same name and grant all privileges

Scroll down a little to see: **Global privileges (Check All /Uncheck All)**
Click: "Check All" in the Global privileges (Check All /Uncheck All).

From the above, our
1. Database name: joomxyz
2. Username: joomxyz
3. Password: user123.

Please note the above parameters because we will soon need them to install our Joomla site.

If you have done everything as specified above, you will have a screenshot as the one shown below.

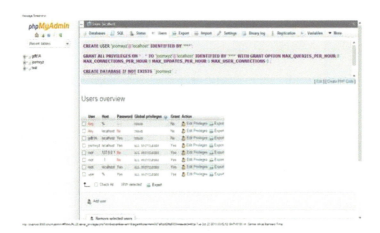

I hope it is phpmyadmin that you are using. If it is, then to make creating a database and its user easier for you, instead of creating the database first before the user and subsequently adding the user to the database, just click on Users...scroll down in the next window and click add user. Choose local as host, then enter the user's name, e.g. joomxyz and a password e.g. user123

Scroll down to see: Database for user 1. Check: Create database with same name and grant all privileges

Scroll down a little to see: Global privileges (Check All /Uncheck All) Click "Check All" in the Global privileges (Check All /Uncheck All).

From the above, our
1. Database name: joomxyz
2. Username: joomxyz
3. Password: user123.

But if you have challenges doing this, just create a database called joomxyz. By default, this database user name is root and its password is blank i.e. it has no password.

So your own parameters will now be
1. Database name: joomxyz
2. Username: root
3. Password: (empty).

Installing Joomla in your computer:

First thing, type http://localhost:8080/ into your browser. The below image will appear.

Name	Last modified	Size	Description
JoomlaTraining/	2013-07-31 21:15	-	
cgi-bin/	2013-10-16 14:58	-	
favicon.ico	2013-01-29 15:18	1.1K	

Powered by AMPPS and Softaculous

Next....Click: JoomlaTraining/ and the image below will appear.

You are expected to enter.
1. Site Name*:
2. Description:
3. Admin Email*:
4. Admin Username*: admin
5. Admin Password*: user123
6. Confirm Admin Password*: user123

Please NOTE: I used admin as Admin Username while user123 as Admin Password. You may use any parameter that is convenient for you. We will use this Admin Username and Password to access the administrator side of the website later on so keep track of them.

Then click NEXT

Database Configuration

Remember our database configuration parameters?

Here they are:
1. Database name: joomxyz
2. Username: joomxyz
3. Password: user123.

We'll use them in the form below:

Filling the Database Configuration:
1. Database type*: Select MySQL
2. Host Name*: Localhost
3. Username*: joomxyz
4. Password*: user123
5. Database*: joomxyz
6. Table prefix*: You may use the one that was randomly generated or enter 3 or 4 alphanumeric characters and MUST end with an underscore (_).
7. Old Database Process*: You may leave the default option that's selected.

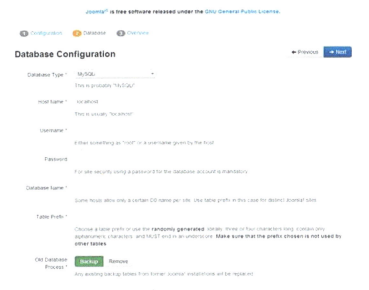

Checking the values we entered so far.

The below image displays all the values we have entered so far in this installation: You don't change anything here.

Click NEXT

Main Configuration

Site Name	My Website
Description	My test website
Site Offline	No
Admin Email	email@email.org
Admin Username	Administrator
Admin Password	......

Database Configuration

Database Type	mysqli
Host Name	localhost
Username	joomla_test
Password	......
Database Name	joomla_test
Table Prefix	joomla_
Old Database Process	Backup

Pre-Installation Check

PHP Version >= 5.3.1	Yes
Magic Quotes GPC Off	Yes
Register Globals Off	Yes
Zlib Compression Support	Yes
XML Support	Yes
Database Support (mysql, pdo, mysqli)	Yes
MB Language is Default	Yes
MB String Overload Off	Yes
INI Parser Support	Yes
JSON Support	Yes
configuration.php Writeable	Yes

Recommended settings:

These settings are recommended for PHP in order to ensure full compatibility with Joomla!
However Joomla! will still operate if your settings do not quite match the recommended configuration.

Directive	Recommended	Actual
Safe Mode	Off	Off
Display Errors	Off	Off
File Uploads	On	On
Magic Quotes Runtime	Off	Off
Output Buffering	Off	On
Session Auto Start	Off	Off
Native ZIP support	On	On

Finalization/Install Sample Data

For the sake of how popular the field of blogging is becoming, we'll choose:

Blog English (GB) Sample Data.

We will now have a blog layout of a website by the time we finish the installation the next window.

Overview
Email Configuration: Leave the selected "NO" since we are not connected to the internet.

Click: INSTALL.

Congratulation, Joomla is now installed.

On this window.

Please click: Remove installation folder.

Here comes our website: Click SITE.

The attached image below explains a few things about the installation

Please note that the items with * are compulsory.

If you have XAMPP already installed. Then access the Joomla file folder in your htdocs in the root directory through the localhost server on your browser and begin the Joomla installation i.e. C://localhost/htdocs/JoomlaTraining. Where JoomlaTraining is the folder where you have your extracted Joomla Files. Your installation will start.

Remember to create your database and its user as you will need those parameters during the installation process.

As for flexibility between Joomla and Wordpress. Wordpress deals more with sites that are content driven like blogs while Joomla is very versatile in creating more complex sites like ecommerce sites, jobs board, social media etc. Joomla can also do content driven sites as well.

Joomla has an edge when it comes to community.

Here is the screenshot of our blog website

So let's continue.....

On this homepage.

Joomla Training is the title of the blog.

You have some articles on the main page.

There are some Menu items (About, Home) to the right of the page and also archived articles etc.

We will discuss how to edit this page as we move to the administrator end of the website.

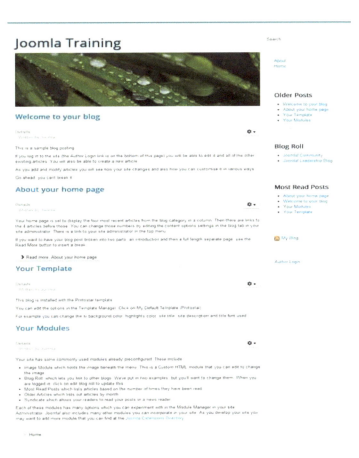

Administrator End

This is the backend, the engine room where a Joomla website is configured.

To access this backend: enter the URL below into your browser:

localhost:8080/JoomlaTraining/administrator

Others may be:

localhost/JoomlaTraining/administrator

However yours is, after entering the above, press Enter. You will be prompted to enter:

1. User Name
2. Password

Remember our Admin User Name and Password during our earlier configuration? Well, here they are:

1. User Name: admin
2. Password: user123.

Now, click LOGIN.

The environment as shown in the image below is the Adminstrator end of a Joomla. Whatever you see in a Joomla website (front end) is done from here.

Take a moment to appreciate this beautiful layout.

Class continues soon...

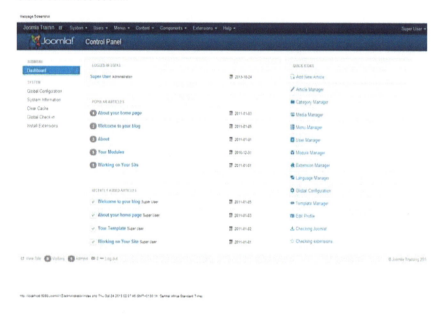

Ok. Let me take your questions one after the other.

1. When I said type: localhost:8080, I was referring to a situatiom whereby Apache returns an error that another application is using port:80.

Originally, to access your localhost is just http://localhost. So in your case, typing localhost/phpmyadmin is also correct instead of localhost:8080/phpmyadmin for those with Apache error on another program using port:8080.

2. The phpmyadmin error you are having maybe as a result of incomplete installation from an incomplete WAMP installation package. Tips: 1. Try uninstall and try to reinstall it. 2. Get a fresh copy from WAMP and install.

Alternatively, get a copy of AMPPS and install, it is more robust.

For those of us using using a localhost on our system, we have been able to install Joomla successfully.

So I want to show those who intend using an online live site to do this training how to set up their own Joomla site.

Installing Joomla on a live site.

These are the steps to be taken.
Caution: Please ensure that your host has a PHP 5.3 and Above* You can see the PHP version in the cpanel of your website.

Let's assume your website name is www.SpringWebHost.com, and the Username of the cpanel is springwe.

1. Create a database called joomxyz. Note as soon as joomxyz is created, it carries the username of the cpanel as a prefix ie springwe_joomxyz.
2. Create a User called trak. This user becomes springwe_trak.
3. Add User springwe_trak to database springwe_joomxyz. Remember to grant all privileges to the User.
4. Upload all the content of your extracted Joomla 3.1 package into the root folder (public_html) of your website. You may use any other folder in your website if you wish.
5. Type your website name into your browser e.g. www.SpringWebHost.com and the Joomla will start immediately.

Refer to a few post above to complete your installation.

3. A tour of the backend (Administrator Panel)

This is where a Joomla site is put together and all the changes are made by the minute when you run a site that requires regular updates.

Since we will be learning most items here let me briefly introduce you to the basic configuration of the administrator's end.

4. Global Configuration

Click Global Configuration on the left side of the Administrator's landing page. It is under SYSTEM.

The Global Configuration setting is grouped into tabbed menu items. They are **Site, System, Server, Permissions, Text Filters.**

The selected item here by default is Site:

Site Setting: You may not need to do much here save you need to change the Site Name or Put the site offline, you may leave other settings as they are. **Metadata Settings** Here you can input some meta tag parameters to optimize your site for search engines. You may also write your Content Rights here.

You can leave any other configuration here (Site) just as it is.

The next tabbed menu item is SYSTEM:
You can leave the configuration for the System just the way it is.

The next tabbed menu item is SERVER:
Here, you can view your database settings. The whole site will stop working if you make any changes here that you are not certain of.
You can as well leave the default settings here just the way they are.

The next tabbed menu item is PERMISSIONS:
You can leave the default settings here just the way they are.

The next tabbed menu item is TEXT FILTERS:
You can leave the default settings here just the way they are.

If you made any changes in the Global Configuration, the click SAVE & CLOSE else click CANCEL to exit this page.

5. Creating Content

Overview of how content is created, managed, and displayed.

Joomla like any other website is driven by content. The Content Manager includes the Article Manager, Category Manager, Featured Articles Manager, and Media Manager.

1. Article Manager
This is usually a text file but you can add images, videos etc. to it. From our homepagehttp://localhost:8080/JoomlaTraining or http://localhost/JoomlaTraining orhttp://YourDomainName.com/JoomlaSiteDirectory as the case may be, you will see the articles vividly displayed. The articles are:

Welcome to your blog
About your home page
Your Template.

We can create new articles or modify the ones we have there already to soothe our purpose. For a start, let us modify the first article on the homepage and then create a new one.

Modifying Welcome to your blog
1. Click Content. On the drop down...
2. Click Article Manager.
All the articles on the site will be displayed here.
Our Article of interest is Welcome to your blog. So click on it.

Now that the article is opened, let's modify it. From the opened window, there are so many parameters to format the article but you need not bother yourself much as most of the configurations here can be left just the way they are so we can discuss just the basics.

Article Title: As the name implies, this is the name of the Article. So let's change it from Welcome to your blog to[b] Welcome to Joomla Training Blog![/b], you may choose any name that is suitable for you. On the main body of the Article, you may change whatever you like.

All the other Tabbed menu items can be left unattended to but if you want to improve the SEO for this Article then click Metadata Options and fill the fields as required.

Click Save & Close. Go to the frontend and refresh your page to see the changes.

To create a new Article.
Click Content
Hover your mouse over Article Manager and click Add New Article.
Click New. Enter the Article Title, the Article content as required and then Click Save & Close.

To view the HTML source code of the Article, click HTML in the formatting tools area (just above the Article content area) of the Article. If you have a pre-formatted Article, you can paste the code here and your Article will be pasted in the content box. Click Save and go to the frontend to view your Article.

2. Category Manager
To access the Category Manager, Click Content, then Category Manager. In this window, there are two Categories created as we installed Joomla, they are: Uncategorised and Blog.
Click on any of them to see its configuration. The major thing here is to change the title of the category, you may as well ignore and create your own new Category. To do so: Click New, enter the Category name and click Save & Close.

Joomla Articles are grouped using the Category Manager. Grouped Articles can be easily accessed by a menu item or a module or can be linked to. On the homepage:

Older Posts houses
Welcome to your blog
About your home page
Your Template
Your Modules

Blog Roll houses
Joomla! Community
Joomla! Leadership Blog.

Putting An Article Into A Category:
Open an Article.
Under *Category, choose the Category you want the Article listed in.

3. Featured Articles Manager
This is used to control which 'Featured Articles are displayed on the Front Page and in what order they are displayed. The Front Page is often the Home page of a web site, but it can be any page in the site. The Front Page is created using a Menu Item with the Front Page layout.

To Feature An Article:
Open an Article. Look at the right side of the page, you will see Details. One of the configurable items listed there is Featured, select Yes.

4. Media Manager
To access the Media Manager, Click Content, on the drop down, and then Click Media Manager. The Media Manager is a tool for uploading or deleting files in the <joomlaroot>/images/ directory on a web server. If you are using a control panel with a file manager, you will find your media files under the 'images' folder.

To upload images to the Media Manager, Click "Upload"...then Click "Choose Files". You will be taken to your computer hard drive to choose files you want to upload and Click "Start Upload". You will have access to these files later if you want to attach them to your Articles, Modules etc.

6. Menus

The Menu Manager manages all the navigation within your Joomla 3.0 website. The default home page, how to display your menus, what is displayed in them. You can have different types of Menu Items. Menu items are created from components installed.

To access the Menu.
Click Menu
In the drop-down, you have Menu Manager, Main Menu and Bottom Menu.

The Menu Manager is used to create New Menus. Main Menu and Bottom Menu were created using the Menu Manager.
Since we have two menu items created for us already, let's pick one of them to see how it works. Our pick is Main Menu.
Click Main Menu: You will notice that two Menu items are listed. They are About and Home.

Click About: This is where this menu item is configured. At the moment we will just be looking at the details configuration of the menu item. You can leave all other configurations just the way they are. Below are our configurable items under "details".
Menu Item Type *:
This tells us the type of item this menu should point to. In this case that we are editing, it points to "Single Article". Click Select close to "Single Article" to see other components that a menu can point to.
Select Article *:
Since our menu item type is Article, we need to select the Article we want to point our menu to. From what is shown, "About" was the Article that was selected. You may Click Select to see other Articles that you can point the menu to.
Status: This is where you can set the Menu item to be Published, Unpublished or Thrashed.
Menu Location: Menu items are attached to a Menu, so you can choose here which of the menus this menu item is attached to.
Parent Item: This is where to choose whether this menu item is a parent item (standalone) or it is a sub menu. By default Menu item Root is selected; that means this menu is a standalone menu. But if this menu is a sub menu or drop down, then select the menu item that this menu is its sub menu.

Click Save & Close.

Create a New Menu Item
Lets create a new menu item that points to an external link to your Facebook Account.
Click Menu...then Main Menu
Click New.
In the "New" opened window, click Select in front of Menu Item Type * to pick the type of component this menu item will point to. In the pop up window, Click System Links, then Choose External URL.
We can now configure our External URL. The configuration here is just like configuring the menu item "about" that we discussed a moment ago except we have to input a Link for this menu item. So let's say our Facebook page URL is http://Facebook.com/SpringWebHost;this URL is now what we will type as our link.
Configure every other item just as we did for "About" menu item.

Adding a New Menu.

Like I earlier said, a Menu houses menu items, so if you have the need to group some menu items under one menu, this is how you can do that. So let's create a Menu called Policies.
Click Menu....hover your mouse over Menu Manager and click Add New Menu. In the window that opened, enter the Menu Title (Policies), Menu Type (Policies), and then the description of the Menu. Click Save & Close.
So whenever you create a New Menu Item, you can select "Policies" if the menu item falls under Policies Menu. Refer: (Menu Location: Menu items are attached to a Menu, so you can choose here which of the menus this menu item is attached to.).

"All the other Tabbed menu items can be left unattended to but if you want to improve the SEO for this Article then click Metadata Options and fill the fields as required."

Please refer to the above on this page.

By the way, take note that:

If you have downloaded Joomla and maybe the name of the Joomla folder you downloaded is Joomla3.25, Just rename it to Joomla3. Duplicate it by copying and renaming others to something like Joomla4, Joomla5 depending on how many sites you want to run. Copy these renamed folders to your www folder if you are using WAMP or to htdocs folder if you are using XAMPP. Remember that you have to create different databases for the Joomla copies you have in your Root Folder.You can access them by Running your WAMP or XAMPP and typing this on your browser: http://localhost/Joomla3 or http://localhost/Joomla4 etc.

2). As per you losing your files in case of a virus attack. Get a working Antivirus (Avast is free) and keep it Updated. Also Download RECUVA, Google it. You can use it to recover files that have been deleted from a hard drive or recycle bin or flash drive. And most importantly, save all your web works (copy the folders) in a flash or hard drive. At least you will only have to reinstall XAMPP or WAMP and copy your folders back in case of you formatting your PC.

3). As for hotel management extension, go to www.joomla.org and search for it in the extensions directory. I think there are premium ones out there for sale that will surely meet your requirements. Some forum online members might even have it. I would have shared it with you if I have one.

7. Components

Components are built to extend Joomla's functionality with third-party options.

To access the Components, Click Components and all the components in your Joomla site will be listed in the drop down.

For the sake of the class let's discuss how to create Contacts, and Joomla! Update.

1. Overview of How to Create a New Contact in Contact Manager

1. Go to Components, then click Contacts. You will be taken to the Contacts Manager window.
2. Click New.
3. Enter New Contact Details, these are basically, email, phone number, address etc.
4. Click Save & Close to See List of your New Contact in Contact Manager.

Let's assume that the contact we just created is titled "Contact Us".

Now let us to create a menu item called Contacts that will point to the "Contact Us" contact.

Here...lets refer to how we created a Menu item before:

Click Menu...then Main Menu......then New

In the "New" opened window, click Select in front of "Menu Item Type *" to pick the type of component this menu item will point to. In the pop up window, click "Contacts"...from the items that slid down. Click "Single Contact".
Click "Select" in front of "Select Contact *" to show and select "Contact Us" from the list.
Enter Contacts as the "Menu Title".

Under the "Advanced Options" tabbed item, Choose "Plain" in "Display Format" i.e. "Advanced Options" --- "Display Format"---"Plain".
With this, when the "Contacts" menu item is clicked at the frontend, the Contact details plus a contact form is displayed.
Click Save & Close. Go and refresh your homepage to see your new menu item called "Contacts".

2. Joomla! Update
Click "Components".....then "Joomla! Update"
In the next window, you will see the message below:

No updates available
You already have the latest Joomla! Version, 3.1.5.

This is because we already have the latest version. If there is an update to Joomla, it show here. With a few clicks, you will be updated to the latest version of Joomla. As a security check, please always ensure that your Joomla version is up to date.

The other components are Joomla defaults, so you may as well leave them the way they are but if need be we can make changes to them later.

8. Modules

Just like the Component, Modules are built to extend Joomla's functionality with third-party options.

To access the "Modules", Click "Extensions" and then "Module Manager", all the "Modules" in your Joomla site will be shown.

The modules shown are the default modules as installed in Joomla and how these modules are positioned in the frontend makes your site appear the way you want it to. So two persons may use the same template but achieve different results.

Creating a New Module
Modules can be created from components installed in Joomla. Or you can install an already made Module. Most of the items we see in the frontend are modules.

So let's create a new module called "User Login" from the installed components in the site. There is a component already installed that we will access to enable us do this task.

Click "Extensions" then "Module Manager".
Click "New". In the next window, click "Login"
Enter a Title for this Module e.g. "User Login"
Click Save & Close.

The module we just created won't appear at the frontend because we did not position it anywhere in the website. I will discuss a concept called "Module Positions" when we get to "Template Manager" shortly.

Module Positions will help us place our "User Login" form in the website. So let's continue to the next topic. We will revisit the "User Login"

9. Plug-in

A plug-in though lighter, has the same function as a Component, Modules; it is built to extend Joomla's functionality with third-party options.

[/b]To access the Plug-ins in our site.[/b]
Click Extensions, then "Plug-in Manager".

Here, all the plug-ins in the system will show. Most plug-ins have very little configurations. You just need to Enable or Disable them. For now, we will not do any Plug-in configuration.

You'll need to be online for some plug-ins to work.

In case of Facebook plug-in, it requires some live data to work.

10. Templates

A template controls the graphical presentation of your website. It determines the layout, colors, type-faces, graphics and other aspects of design that make your site unique. There are two types of
templates: "Site template" for front-end presentation and "Administrator template" for back-end presentation.

To view your templates....Go to "Extensions" => "Template Manager". The window below will appear.

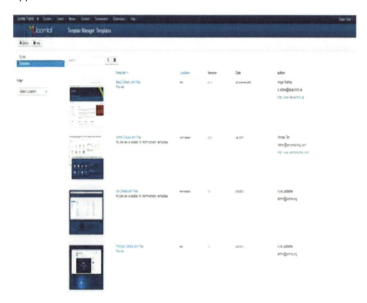

Site Template
The site templates change the way your website looks to visitors.

Most of the time, you will be dealing with the site templates to change public look-n-feel of your website. Below is an example of a Site template, it is Joomla's default blog template.

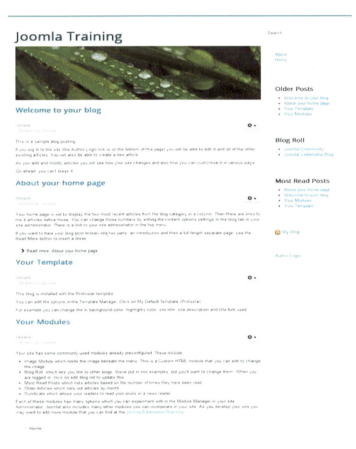

Administrator template

Administrator templates changes the way the administrator interface looks.

If you are building a website for yourself, then you will probably never need to change your back-end template. When building websites for clients, you might need to slightly customize the administrator template to reflect your customer's brand. Below is a screen shot of an Administrator template.

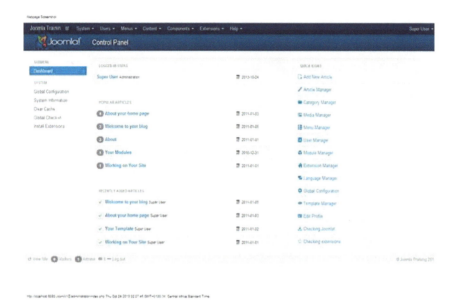

Template Resources
The quickest and easiest way to enhance the design of your website is to use an existing Joomla template. There are many available on the internet.

Free Templates Resources
The Joomla community creates thousands of free templates for you to choose from. Check following websites:
http://www.joomla24.com
http://www.joomlaos.de/
http://www.bestofjoomla.com.

Commercial Templates Resources
If you have enough budget to purchase a template, then we strongly recommend you take a look at following template providers.
http://www.joomlashine.com
http://www.joomlart.com
http://www.rockettheme.com
http://www.yootheme.com
http://www.gavick.com

Searching on the Internet
You can search on Google with the key words: "Joomla Templates" or "template for Joomla" and you will get over 120 million results!

Module Position

A module performs simple tasks and displays content as small blocks positioned around the page. Each module is located in a specific position, e.g. module "Main menu" is placed in position "position-7". Each position is designed to occupy a place in a page's layout, i.e. position "position-8" is placed on the left side of main content. Each template can have many different positions occupying various places on the page.

To Preview Module Positions, you need to enable "Preview Module Positions"
1. Go to "Extensions" => "Template Manager" => "Options"
2. Next, set the parameter "Preview Module Positions" to "Enabled" and click "Save & Close"
3. Enable the preview of the module positions in the template by appending "?tp=1" to the web address. This means type: http://localhost/JoomlaTraining/?tp=1 on your browser and press enter. Please refresh the page after changing this setting and you will have your site loaded with its module positions just like you have in the image below.

Now you can see all module positions of the template. This will help you to choose the right position when you add a new module.

What you need to do as an assignment is to position our "Login Form" into any position of your choice.

Joomla Training

Position: position-1 | Style: none outline

Position: banner | Style: xhtml outline

Position: position-8 | Style: xhtml outline | Position: position-3 | Style: xhtml outline

Position: position-7 | Style: well outline

About
Home
Contacts

Welcome to your blog

Details
Written by Joomla

This is a sample blog posting

If you log in to the site (the Author Login link is on the bottom of this page) you will be able to edit it and all of the other existing articles. You will also be able to create a new article.

As you add and modify articles you will see how your site changes and also how you can customise it in various ways.

Go ahead, you can't break it

About your home page

Details
Written by Joomla

Your home page is set to display the four most recent articles from the blog category in a column. Then there are links to the 4 articles before those. You can change those numbers by editing the content options settings in the blog tab in your site administrator. There is a link to your site administrator in the top menu

If you want to have your blog post broken into two parts, an introduction and then a full length separate page, use the Read More button to insert a break

> Read more: About your home page

Your Template

Details
Written by Joomla

This blog is installed with the Protostar template

You can edit the options in the Template Manager. Click on My Default Template (Protostar)

For example you can change the si background color, highlights color, site title site description and title font used

Your Modules

Details
Written by Joomla

Your site has some commonly used modules already preconfigured. These include:

- Image Module which holds the image beneath the menu. This is a Custom HTML module that you can edit to change the image
- Blog Roll which lets you link to other blogs. We've put in two examples but you'll want to change them. When you are logged in, click on edit blog roll to update this.
- Most Read Posts which lists articles based on the number of times they have been read.
- Older Articles which lists out articles by month
- Syndicate which allows your readers to read your posts in a news reader

Each of these modules has many options which you can experiment with in the Module Manager in your site Administrator. Joomla! also includes many other modules you can incorporate in your site. As you develop your site you may want to add more module that you can find at the Joomla Extensions Directory

Position: position-7 | Style: well outline

Older Posts

- Welcome to your blog
- About your home page
- Your Template
- Your Modules

Position: position-7 | Style: well outline

Blog Roll

- Joomla! Community
- Joomla! Leadership Blog

Position: position-7 | Style: well outline

Most Read Posts

- About your home page
- Welcome to your blog
- Your Modules
- Your Template

Position: position-7 | Style: well outline

My Blog

Position: position-7 | Style: well outline

Author Login

Position: position-2 | Style: none outline

Home

11. Extension Manager

Default Joomla extensions are good for a start, but in the long run they are just not enough. As your website evolves, you will want to add more functionality that goes beyond these default extensions.

The best place for you to find useful Joomla extensions is Joomla Extensions Directory (JED) i.e. http://joomla.org/extensions. It is a large resource with a large number of Joomla extensions divided into certain categories based on functionality. Or you can search the internet for any Joomla extension you want.

To Add Extensions
1. Go to "Extensions" => "Extension Manager"
2. Next, click the "Choose File" button to select the Joomla extension package you downloaded
3. After that, click "Upload & Install" to start uploading and install this file to your site.

Joomla automatically knows the right place to put the extension based on its type. For instance, if the extension is a component, you will see it in the menu "Components", if that extension is a module; you will find it in "Module Manager" and so on.

So look for the installed Extension, configure it as specified by the the Extension, and put it in the Module Position of your choice.

I installed Joomla 3.1 in the link below, you can use it for your practice.

Site URL: http://joomlaextended.com/demo3.
Administrator: http://joomlaextended.com/demo3/administrator
Username: demo
Password: demo.

Users

Joomla allows your website to have multiple registered users. All users are arranged in user groups, which have permission to access certain parts of the website. By default these are the user groups:

|—Guest
|—Manager
|—|—Administrator
|—Registered
|—|—Author
|—|—|—Editor
|—|—|—|—Publisher
|—Super Users

Users assigned to "Super Users" group can work in both back-end and front-end
Users assigned to "Registered" group can work only at the front-end.

You can manage users, user groups and access levels in the menu "Users".

Add A User
Click Users ---> User Manager ---> Add New User.
Enter the User details in the Account Details Tab. Remember to Assign the User to a Group in the "Assigned User Groups" tab.

12. Media Manager
Here you can upload files that you will need to use in your website. If you want to attach images to your "Articles" or "Custom HTML Module", you can create upload files by following this link.

1. Go to "Content" ---> "Media Manager"
2. Click "Upload"
3. Click "Choose Files". You will then be taken to your computer hard drive to choose the files you want to upload.
4. Click "Start Upload"
These files will be uploaded to the "images" folder in your Joomla files directory. But if you need to group your files into folders, follow the
instructions below.

Creating a Folder
1. Go to "Content" ---> "Media Manager"
2. Click "Create New Folder", "Input a folder name e.g. "TrainingFiles" and click the "Create Folder" button.

Now you have your new folder called "TrainingFiles" in the Media Manager.

Uploading Files
Now, it is time to upload the files into your newly created files folder "TrainingFiles".
1. Click on the "TrainingFiles" folder,
2. Click "Upload"
3. Click "Choose Files". You will then be taken to your computer hard drive to choose the files you want to upload.
4. Click "Start Upload"

These files will be uploaded to the "TrainingFile" folder.

To select multiple files. You can use your mouse cursor to mark all files or hold the "CTRL" key and click on the individual files you want to select, to mark them and Click "Start Upload".

13. Language Manager
Go to "Extensions" ---> "Language Manager"
Here, you will see all the languages installed in your Joomla site. In this site, we have only one language installed which is
English (United Kingdom). You can install other languages as you wish.

14. SEO & SEF

For a basic class such as this, you can optimize your website to be search engine friendly by following the following steps:

1. Go to "System" ---> "Global Configurations".
---**Under SEO Settings:**
Click "YES" for Search Engine Friendly URLs.
---**Under Metadata Settings:**
"Site Meta Description": Enter a description of the overall Web site that is to be used by search engines. Generally, a maximum of 20 words is optimal.
"Site Meta Keywords": Enter the keywords and phrases that best describe your Web site. Separate keywords and phrases with a comma.
"Content Rights": Describe what rights others have to use this content.

2. Click Save & Close.
You can use other methods to promote you website as well.

15. Security

Here are some steps to secure your Joomla website.

1. Website backup: Have a back of your website from time to time. Do rely on your host to do it for you, do it yourself!

2. Infested computer: Malware, spyware and other computer infections account for vast majority of websites hack. Please ensure that your computer is infections free
because you may be uploading infested files from your computer if it is not free, thereby making your website vulnerable to attacks.

3. Old unused extensions: If you are not making use of any extension, please delete it now!

4. Badly coded third party extensions: Please read the review of all of your third party extensions before you install them into your website.

5. Cheap/Free Host. Some cheap and free hosting company cramp very many websites together, and if any website in that server is attacked, all other websites in the
server may be infected.

6. Restrict user's privileges: If you have a forum or allow uploads for any reason, please set restrictions on the file types, file sizes and in your .htaccess file,
use clever coding to detect common exploit terms.

7. Keep Joomla core files up to date: Please ensure that you are running the latest version of Joomla at all times, keep your extensions up to date as well.

8. Weak Joomla Administrator Password: First rename the Administrator's username from admin to something you can remember. Then choose a password that is a combination
of different characters.

9. Giving away your Joomla login information: If you are soliciting for support, please ensure whom you are dealing with before letting go of your login details.

10. No security measure for a Joomla website: Database prefix, super admin ID, upload limit, blocking terms in URLs, block all SQL injections. Some of these are basic, some are complicated and should be done by a Joomla professional.

From my point of view, if you are a serious business person and you have not implemented these and other Joomla security measures, you are begging to be hacked and being ridiculed. I have been there, it is not a palatable place to be.

Now that we have successfully completed the table of content listed at the beginning of this tutorial, we will now learn how to move our website from our Localhost in our computer to the internet.

There are a few steps we will take to achieve this, they are:
1. Configure the configuration.php file
2. Upload all your localhost website files to your online website using FTP.
3. Export your database from phpmyadmin in you localhost
4. Import your database into your online website.
5. Check your website in your browser.

Moving From Localhost to the Internet

1. Configure the configuration.php file
Open your Joomla website folder, look for configuration.php, open it. If you have followed this class step-by-step so far, your configuration.php file will look like what we have below. Not familiar with codes? There is nothing to worry about, you just need to alter four lines here.

The configuration.php file is better viewed using Notepad ++. You can download Notepad ++ from http://notepad-plus-plus.org/download. It is free.

Now that you have your Notepad ++, open the configuration.php file using Notepad ++.

Here is my configuration.php.

```php
<?php
class JConfig {
public $offline = '0';
public $offline_message = 'This site is down for maintenance.<br /> Please check back again
soon.';
public $display_offline_message = '1';
public $offline_image = '';
public $sitename = 'Joomla Training';
public $editor = 'tinymce';
public $captcha = '0';
public $list_limit = '20';
```

```php
public $access = '1';
public $debug = '0';
public $debug_lang = '0';
public $dbtype = 'mysqli';
public $host = 'localhost';
public $user = 'gdft1A';
public $password = 'admin';
public $db = 'gdft1A';
public $dbprefix = 'gsixm_';
public $live_site = '';
public $secret = 'oP06WEO4zMxnUYrN';
public $gzip = '0';
public $error_reporting = 'default';
public $helpurl =
'http://help.joomla.org/proxy/index.php?option=com_help&amp;keyref=Help{major}{minor}:{keyref}';
public $ftp_host = '';
public $ftp_port = '';
public $ftp_user = '';
public $ftp_pass = '';
public $ftp_root = '';
public $ftp_enable = '';
public $offset = 'UTC';
public $mailer = 'mail';
public $mailfrom = 'info@joomlaclassics.com';
public $fromname = 'Joomla Training';
public $sendmail = '/usr/sbin/sendmail';
public $smtpauth = '0';
public $smtpuser = '';
public $smtppass = '';
public $smtphost = 'localhost';
public $smtpsecure = 'none';
public $smtpport = '25';
public $caching = '0';
public $cache_handler = 'file';
public $cachetime = '15';
public $MetaDesc = '';
public $MetaKeys = '';
public $MetaTitle = '1';
public $MetaAuthor = '1';
public $MetaVersion = '0';
public $robots = '';
public $sef = '1';
public $sef_rewrite = '0';
public $sef_suffix = '0';
public $unicodeslugs = '0';
public $feed_limit = '10';
public $log_path = 'C:\\Program Files (x86)\\Ampps\\www\\JoomlaTraining/logs';
public $tmp_path = 'C:\\Program Files (x86)\\Ampps\\www\\JoomlaTraining/tmp';
public $lifetime = '15';
```

public $session_handler = 'database';
}

We are going to make changes to the bolded lines above to reflect changes that our site require to be able to run online.

Before you proceed, please have a backup of the configuration.php file.

We will make assumptions here, let's say our website is http://JoomlaExtended.com. When the website was hosted, it was given a username by the hosting company, and let's say the username is "joomlaex". We will use this username "joomlaex" as a suffix followed by an underscore (_) to our database name and it's Username. This means:

public $user = 'gdft1A'; becomes **public $user = 'joomlaex_gdft1A';.** This is for the Username

public $db = 'gdft1A'; becomes **public $db = 'joomlaex_gdft1A';,** This is for the Database.

Changing "log" and "temp" folders paths
In my computer, I installed Joomla in this path: C:\\Program Files (x86)\\Ampps\\www\\ as shown in the configuration.php file, so since we are moving the website online to my domain name http://JoomlaExtended.com; C:\\Program Files (x86)\\Ampps\\www\\ will then be replaced by "/home/joomlaex/public_html/". This means:

public $log_path = 'C:\\Program Files (x86)\\Ampps\\www\\JoomlaTraining/logs';becomes **public $log_path = '/home/joomlaex/public_html/logs';**

public $tmp_path = 'C:\\Program Files (x86)\\Ampps\\www\\JoomlaTraining/tmp';becomes **public $tmp_path = '/home/joomlaex/public_html/tmp';**

Our New configuration.php file will now be:

```
<?php
class JConfig {
public $offline = '0';
public $offline_message = 'This site is down for maintenance.<br /> Please check back again soon.';
public $display_offline_message = '1';
public $offline_image = '';
public $sitename = 'Joomla Training';
public $editor = 'tinymce';
public $captcha = '0';
public $list_limit = '20';
public $access = '1';
public $debug = '0';
public $debug_lang = '0';
public $dbtype = 'mysqli';
```

```
public $host = 'localhost';
public $user = 'joomlaex_gdft1A';
public $password = 'admin';
public $db = 'joomlaex_gdft1A';
public $dbprefix = 'gsixm_';
public $live_site = '';
public $secret = 'oP06WEO4zMxnUYrN';
public $gzip = '0';
public $error_reporting = 'default';
public $helpurl =
'http://help.joomla.org/proxy/index.php?option=com_help&amp;keyref=Help{major}{minor}:{keyref}';
public $ftp_host = '';
public $ftp_port = '';
public $ftp_user = '';
public $ftp_pass = '';
public $ftp_root = '';
public $ftp_enable = '';
public $offset = 'UTC';
public $mailer = 'mail';
public $mailfrom = 'info@joomlaclassics.com';
public $fromname = 'Joomla Training';
public $sendmail = '/usr/sbin/sendmail';
public $smtpauth = '0';
public $smtpuser = '';
public $smtppass = '';
public $smtphost = 'localhost';
public $smtpsecure = 'none';
public $smtpport = '25';
public $caching = '0';
public $cache_handler = 'file';
public $cachetime = '15';
public $MetaDesc = '';
public $MetaKeys = '';
public $MetaTitle = '1';
public $MetaAuthor = '1';
public $MetaVersion = '0';
public $robots = '';
public $sef = '1';
public $sef_rewrite = '0';
public $sef_suffix = '0';
public $unicodeslugs = '0';
public $feed_limit = '10';
public $log_path = '/home/joomlaex/public_html/logs';
public $tmp_path = '/home/joomlaex/public_html/tmp';
public $lifetime = '15';
public $session_handler = 'database';
}
```

Please save the file.

2. Upload all your localhost website files to your online website using FTP.
Using an FTP program such as Filezilla, upload all your website files to the public_html folder in your online website.

3. Export your database from phpmyadmin in you localhost
a. Open http://localhost.com/phpmyadmin
b. Click the database name: gdft1A
c. Click Export
d. Click OK.
The database "gdft1A" will be downloaded into your computer as "gdft1A.sql"

4. Import your database into your online website.
a. Log into your online control panel(cpanel)
b. Click MySQL Databases and create a database named "gdft1A" and Username: "gdft1A". Remember to Add User "gdft1A" to Database "gdft1A". Grant all privileges to the User.
c. Go back to the Cpanel Home. Under "Databases", Click "phpmyadmin"
d. Click on the database named "gdft1A"
e. Click "import"
f. Under "File to Import:" Click "Choose File". Look for "gdft1A.sql" in your computer and select it
g. Scroll down to Click "GO". Your database "gdft1A.sql" that you downloaded will be imported into "gdft1A". You do not have to do anything again here.

5. Check your website in your browser.
That is to say you should type your website address e.g. http://JoomlaExtended.com in your browser and press enter.

If you have followed the 5 steps outlined above, your website will start running just as it was in your localhost.

You can now log into your website's administrator end e.g. http://JoomlaExtended.com/administrator to continue configuring your website to your taste.

QUESTION LAYOUT
I installed Joomla! on my hosting server then, I downloaded a Joomla! template which I saw as free and responsive and I loved the layout of the template as shown by the demo after that, I logged on to my backend as a super user, then I uploaded and installed the new template through the extensions directory and activated it as default for my site front end from the templates manager after which I uninstalled previous Joomla! default templates.

My Questions
1. Why is the layout I am seeing on my website front end after activating the template from my back end different from what I saw on the demo before I downloaded the template?

2. How can I make my website front end look exactly like the template demo I saw. What are those things I need to change, activate or enable or what do I do?

3. Under the "Extensions Manager > Manage," some items, components, modules and plugins are locked or have a small lock key beside them and gives me this error "User State Not Permitted" when I click on it or try to enable it. How do I unlock it or use those locked items? Do they have an adverse effect on my website if tampered with?

Questions 1 and 2 have the same answer.
There are two types of templates. One is "Template Only" while the other one is "Quickstart Template".

"Quickstart Template" contains all the Joomla files, the template owner's components, modules, plugins, images, videos etc. or any other third party extensions. This is what you'll upload into your website to make it look exactly like the demo you saw. You need an FTP program to upload the "Quickstart Template". It is uploaded just the way you upload Joomla files into your website. Make sure you **Install Sample Data** during your installation process.

Question 3.
The extension with "User State Not Permitted" is a protected extension, part of the core of Joomla and deliberately protected from tampering! If you need to use that extension, you need to create another instance of it so you can do whatever you want with it, though not all the protected extensions can be created from the Module menus.

I hope those helped.

1. Quickstart Templates are comprehensive, some as high as 80MB. Quickstart is like your initial Joomla installation. Instead of installing Joomla files, you just install the Quickstart pack, it contains all the Joomla files and many more. Most template providers give a Quickstart template. If the template is responsive, the template inside the Quickstart will also be responsive.

2. Please note: Quickstart template is not an extension, it is not a template. It cannot be installed as an extension. Quickstart template is another word for the demo you saw online. So if you are installing a Quickstart template, it means you are installing the demo.

3. If you want to use a Quickstart template, YOU DON'T INSTALL JOOMLA AT ALL. Just install the files in the Quickstart template, it contains all in the initial Joomla files and other third party extensions.

www.ingramcontent.com/pod-product-compliance
Lightning Source LLC
Chambersburg PA
CBHW041147050326
40689CB00001B/523